THE
BURGER
BOOK

OTHER BOOKS BY HONEY AND LARRY ZISMAN INCLUDE

The 47 Best Chocolate Chip Cookies in the World
Super Sweets
The Great American Peanut Butter Book
The Great International Dessert Cookbook

c

THE
BURGER
BOOK

More than
95
delicious
and
ingenious
ways
to enjoy
the juicy
pleasures of
hamburgers,
plus
27
perfect
side-dish
recipes for
potatoes,
relishes,
salads, and
shakes

Honey and Larry Zisman

St. Martin's Press · New York

DESIGNED BY BARBARA MARKS

Library of Congress Cataloging in Publication Data

Zisman, Larry.
    The burger book.

    1. Cookery (Beef) 2. Sandwiches.
3. Menus.
I. Zisman, Honey. II. Title.
TX749.Z57   1987   641.6′62   86-27907
ISBN 0-312-00084-7 (pbk.)

First Edition
10 9 8 7 6 5 4 3 2 1

In a 1970 CBS television broadcast, Charles Kuralt talked about hamburgers and America:

Americans ate 40 billion burgers last year, give or take a few hundred million, and on the road you tend to eat more than your share. You can find your way across this country using burger joints the way a navigator uses stars. . . . We have munched Bridge Burgers in the shadow of Brooklyn Bridge and Cable Burgers hard by the Golden Gate, Dixie Burgers in the sunny South and Yankee Doodle Burgers in the North. The Civil War must be over—they taste exactly alike. . . . We had a Capitol Burger—guess where. And so help us, in the inner courtyard of the Pentagon, a Penta Burger.

But this is not merely a local phenomenon. The smell of fried onions is abroad in the land, and if the French chefs among us will avert their eyes, we will finish reciting our menu of the last few weeks on the highways of America. We've had Grabba Burgers, Kinga Burgers, Lotta Burgers, Castle Burgers, Country Burgers, Bronco Burgers, Broadway Burgers, Broiled Burgers, Beefnut Burgers, Bell Burgers, Plush Burgers, Prime Burgers, Flame Burgers . . . Dude Burgers, Char Burgers, Tall Boy Burgers, Golden Burgers, 747 Jet Burgers, Whiz Burgers, Nifty Burgers, and Thing Burgers. . . .

CONTENTS

THE GREATEST TOWER OF THEM ALL   xi

SUGGESTIONS FOR EATING THE BEST
HAMBURGER POSSIBLE   xii

BURGERS

YOUR BASIC BURGERS   1

TIP-TOP TOPPINGS
FOR YOUR BASIC BURGER   5

FAMOUS BURGERS   9

THE BEST BEEF BURGERS   21

SPECIALTY BURGERS   59

THE EXTRAS

ROLLS   73

SALADS AND SIDES   79

RELISHES AND KETCHUP   97

DRINKS   103

INDEX   109

All hail the man named Sam,
Who loved the burgers comma ham.
  Such was his task,
  Always to ask,
Have you burgers: beef, pork, or lamb?

THE GREATEST TOWER OF THEM ALL

You have read in the Book of Genesis, 11:1-9, of course, of the Tower of Babel built in Babylonia by the descendants of Noah after the Great Flood in a presumptuous effort to reach heaven.

Who has not heard of the Leaning Tower of Pisa, in the Tuscany region of north-central Italy?

On the north bank of the Thames is the Tower of London, not a tower, really, but interesting nevertheless as an ancient fortress, a royal residence, a jail for illustrious prisoners, and a museum displaying the crown jewels, still guarded by Beefeaters.

Mention Paris and one immediately pictures the Eiffel Tower, a symbol of the French capital for nearly one hundred years since its construction for the Paris Exposition of 1889.

Think of the magnificent view of Chicago from the top of the Sears Tower, the tallest building in the world with 110 floors and a height of 1,454 feet.

Now visualize the All-American Hamburger Tower, a stack of all the beef patties eaten in just one year in the United States. It rises an incredible, an astonishing, an almost unbelievable 450,000 miles into the sky, nearly twice the distance from the earth to the moon.

Can there be any doubt that the All-American Hamburger Tower is the greatest tower of them all?

If, however, heights make you dizzy, think instead of all those hamburgers forming a wall-to-wall carpet, completely covering Manhattan Island in a rug four burgers thick.

And finally, for those of you interested in hamburger chains—and we do not mean McDonald's or Burger King—if all the hamburgers eaten in the United States in one year were placed side by side, they would form a chain 1,800,000 miles long. That is long enough to circle the earth seventy-two times at the Equator.

That, surely, is the biggest chain of hamburgers anywhere.

SUGGESTIONS FOR EATING
THE BEST HAMBURGER POSSIBLE

- There are generally four different kinds of meat used for hamburger: ground beef, ground chuck, ground round, and ground sirloin. Ground beef is the least expensive and has the highest fat content. Ground chuck has less fat but costs more, while ground round is leaner yet and carries even an higher price tag. Ground sirloin is the leanest and most expensive of the four.

- Ground meat with a higher fat content can be used when cooking on a grill or when the hamburgers can be drained. Leaner meat is preferred when the hamburgers are cooked right in the pan with other ingredients or a sauce.

- Meat that is ground twice will give denser, more compact hamburgers but they will have a finer texture.

- According to your tastes, other types of ground meat, such as lamb, pork, and veal, can be substituted for beef when making hamburgers.

- When selecting ground meat in the store, make sure that the package feels cold and that it is not torn or open.

- Do not take ground meat from the refrigerated case in the store while you still have other shopping to do. Select the hamburger meat after you have finished your other shopping and just before heading to the checkout counter.

- It is normal for store-wrapped fresh ground meat to be a rich red on the outside and a darker color on the inside. This difference in coloring is caused by the lack of air in the tightly wrapped package. The overall bright color will return if the meat is left unwrapped in the refrigerator for a short time.

- Hamburger meat should not be kept in the refrigerator for more than a day or two. It can be stored in the freezer for up to three months.

- When making raw hamburgers that will be frozen, shape meat very lightly into patties. If freezing patties individually, wrap first in plastic wrap and then freezer paper. When several patties are frozen together in one package, separate them with a double layer of wax paper before wrapping. Be sure to squeeze out as much air as possible from the package.

- Do not add seasonings to the meat before freezing, since the flavors of the seasonings can change while frozen. Cooked hamburgers can be frozen, but the seasonings might taste slightly different when defrosted.

- When defrosting frozen hamburger meat, let the meat sit in the refrigerator still wrapped in the package from the freezer. Do not defrost hamburger meat by letting it sit out on the kitchen counter.

- Do not refreeze hamburger meat after it has thawed.

- When making patties from ground meat that was frozen in bulk (not formed into patties before freezing), blot patties with a paper towel to remove excess moisture.

- It is easiest to use a fork, rather than fingers or a spoon, to blend other ingredients into ground meat when making hamburgers.

- Handle ground meat as little as possible when forming it into hamburger patties. The less the meat is handled, the more tender and juicy the hamburgers will be. Hamburgers that are handled too much become more compact and turn out to be tougher and drier after being cooked.

- When cooking fresh hamburgers in a pan or on a grill, make sure that the pan or the grill is very hot before placing the hamburgers on it. Quickly brown both sides and then cook one side completely before turning over. Do not press down with a spatula or turn the burgers more than once (except for frozen patties) to ensure that they will be as tender and juicy as possible.

- When cooking frozen hamburgers in a pan, heat the pan so it is very hot and quickly brown the patties on both sides, then lower heat and continue cooking, turning two or three times. When broiling frozen hamburgers, set the broiling pan further away from heat than you normally set it for cooking fresh burgers.

- You can get a general idea of how much a hamburger has cooked by checking the edges. If the edges are still red, the hamburger is very rare; browned edges mean the hamburger is medium; and charred edges indicate that it is well done. It is necessary, however, to cut into the hamburger to find out exactly how much the inside has cooked. Make as small a cut as possible to avoid losing too much of the juices.

- When barbecuing hamburgers on an outdoor grill, a nice smoky flavor can be obtained by adding a few damp chips of apple wood, hickory wood, or mesquite wood to the coals. You can also get a smoky flavor when cooking hamburgers indoors by adding a small amount of liquid smoke to the ground meat before shaping it into patties. Liquid smoke is a natural and safe product made by condensing the smoke from burning hickory wood into a concentrate.

For people who are reluctant to travel outside of the United States because they do not know how to ask for a hamburger in a foreign language, here is a listing (obtained through the assistance of foreign embassies, consulates, and missions to the United Nations) of the word for "hamburger" in twenty-three other languages. In many cases the word for "hamburger" is easy to remember since it is the same as in English.

Arabic	hamburger	Iranian	hamburger
Chinese	hanpao	Italian	amburgo
Danish	hamburger	Japanese	hamburger
Dutch	hamburger	Norwegian	hamburger
Finnish	hampurilainen	Polish	hamburger,
French	hamburger		kotlet mielony
German	hamburger	Portuguese	hamburgo
Greek	bifteki	Russian	buterbrod
Hebrew	hamburger	South African	hamburger
Hungarian	hamburger	Spanish	hamburguesa
Icelandic	hamborgari	Swedish	hamburgare
Indian	hamburger,	Yugoslavian	pljeskavica
	cutlets		

Your Basic Burgers

YOUR BASIC BURGER

2 pounds ground beef
Salt to taste
1¹/₂ teaspoons onion powder
¹/₄ teaspoon pepper

The National Dairy Board ran a "Win a Cheeseburger Party Sweepstakes" in which contestants had to pick their favorite cheeseburger from six different kinds of cheese toppings:

- Blue cheese
- Muenster cheese
- Swiss cheese
- Monterey Jack
- Cheddar
- Mozzarella

Two hundred lucky first-prize winners received a complete party set, which included a kettle grill, a TV set, plastic dish and glass set, chef's hat and apron, condiment cart, barbecue tools, and a $10 check for buying ground beef and cheese to make their own favorite cheeseburger.

Using a fork, gently mix meat, salt, onion powder, and pepper. Shape into 6 patties, handling meat as little as possible and taking care not to press meat together tightly.

Broil, grill, or pan-fry the patties. The length of cooking time will depend upon whether you and your guests like your hamburgers rare, medium, or well done.

Yield: 6 burgers

YOUR BASIC CHEESEBURGER

2 pounds ground beef
Salt to taste
1 1/2 teaspoons onion powder
1/4 teaspoon pepper
6 slices cheese of your choice

Using a fork, gently mix meat, salt, onion powder, and pepper. Shape into 6 patties, handling meat as little as possible and taking care not to press meat together tightly.

Broil, grill, or pan-fry the patties. The length of cooking time will depend upon whether you and your guests like your cheeseburgers rare, medium, or well done.

A minute or two before the cheeseburgers are done cooking, place slices of cheese on top, cover, and continue cooking until cheese has melted.

Yield: 6 burgers

BACON-CHEESEBURGER

If desired, arrange 2 slices of cooked bacon on top of each nearly cooked patty (see recipe above) before placing cheese on top.

Cheeseburgers are serious business. The august *New York Times* published an article in September 1983, chronicling one man's twenty-five-year search for the perfect cheeseburger, a quest that has taken him throughout the United States as well as to exotic foreign spots like Paris and Cam Ranh Bay, Vietnam.

Although writer Andrew H. Malcolm found several cheeseburgers to which he gave 9 1/2 buns out of a perfect rating of 10 buns, his search for the perfect cheeseburger still goes on.

TIP-TOP TOPPINGS FOR YOUR BASIC BURGER

Your Basic Burger is already perfect served all by itself or on a roll, but for an extra treat, try these Tip-Top Toppings:

- Mayonnaise, a thick slice of tomato, a thin slice of Bermuda onion, and lettuce
- Creamed spinach, a thin slice of ham, and crumbled blue cheese
- Crushed garlic clove, softened butter or margarine, paprika, and blue cheese mixed together
- Liver pâté and a thin slice of onion
- Bacon slices and a sliced hard-boiled egg
- Cottage cheese, chopped watercress, and alfalfa sprouts
- Stewed tomatoes and grated Romano cheese
- Sauerkraut, thin slices of salami, and hot and sweet mustard
- Peanut butter and alfalfa sprouts
- Creamed corn and chopped sweet pickles
- Sour cream, chopped chives, and sliced cucumber
- Mozzarella cheese, bacon, and sliced black olives
- Cream cheese mixed with caviar
- Shredded Gruyère cheese and a dash of nutmeg
- Tuna fish and chopped parsley mixed with mayonnaise
- Bologna, sliced green olives, and creamy Italian salad dressing
- Tomato sauce and anchovies
- Yogurt, apple slices, and a dash of cinnamon
- Shredded carrots, raisins, and a dollop of mayonnaise
- Chutney with a dash of curry
- Lettuce, onion slices, and Thousand Island dressing

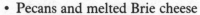

- Pecans and melted Brie cheese
- Orange slices, fresh mint leaves, and a dollop of sour cream
- Escarole lettuce, sliced radishes, and yogurt
- Chutney and melted Colby cheese
- Cold cooked shrimp, lettuce, and horseradish
- Crab meat, celery leaves, and a dash of lemon juice
- Melted Gruyère cheese, tomato slices, and cucumber slices
- Guacamole and tortilla chips
- Sautéed mushrooms, green peppers, and onions
- Chopped radishes, chopped parsley, and sour cream
- A slice of orange and a dash of nutmeg
- Chopped, cooked scallops and tartar sauce
- Softened butter or margarine, tarragon, and crushed garlic clove
- Mashed avocado, lemon juice, one or two drops of Tabasco sauce, and shredded sharp Cheddar cheese
- Canadian bacon, Muenster cheese, and mustard
- Cooked zucchini slices, tomato slices, and grated Parmesan cheese
- Drained marinated artichoke hearts and French dressing
- Sliced ham, honey, and mustard

FAMOUS
BURGERS

HAMBURG STEAKS

One of the earliest recipes for hamburger appeared in Fannie Farmer's classic cookbook THE ORIGINAL BOSTON COOKING-SCHOOL COOK BOOK 1896. Ms. Farmer's recipe was as follows:

Chop finely one pound lean raw beef; season lightly with salt, pepper, and a few drops onion juice or one-half shallot finely chopped. Shape, cook, and serve as Meat Cakes. A few gratings of nutmeg and one egg slightly beaten may be added.

NOTE: Fannie Farmer's hamburg steaks are as good today as they were nearly one-hundred years ago.

"Hamburg Steaks" recipe from *The Original Boston Cooking-School Cook Book 1896* by Fannie Merritt Farmer (Copyright 1896 by Fannie Merritt Farmer), published by Weathervane Books, a division of Imprint Society, Inc. Used with permission of Hugh Lauter Levin Associates, New York.

CRAIG CLAIBORNE'S HAMBURGERS

1 1/2 pounds ground round steak
Salt
Freshly ground black pepper
4 tablespoons butter
1 teaspoon Worcestershire sauce
1/4 cup chopped parsley
Juice of 1/2 lemon

1. Divide the meat into four portions and shape each portion into a round patty. Handle the meat lightly, pressing just enough so that it holds together. Sprinkle the bottom of a heavy skillet with a very light layer of salt and heat the skillet until very hot. Add the patties and sear well on one side. Using a pancake turner, turn the patties quickly and reduce the heat. Cook to the desired degree of doneness, 3 minutes or longer.

2. When the hamburgers are done, sprinkle them with salt and pepper and top each patty with 1 tablespoon of butter. Transfer the hamburgers to a hot serving platter and sprinkle with Worcestershire sauce, parsley and lemon juice. Serve on buttered toast or on toasted buns.

Yield: 4 servings

From *Craig Claiborne's Kitchen Primer,* used with permission.

One 5 1/2-ounce hamburger made from lean beef supplies the complete daily protein requirement for a woman and about two-thirds of the daily requirement for a man.

In addition, that same hamburger provides the following percentages of vitamins and minerals of an adult's Recommended Daily Allowances:

- 11% thiamine
- 21% riboflavin
- 29% niacin
- 18% B-6
- 73% B-12
- 11% magnesium
- 23% iron
- 76% zinc.

CALIFORNIA BURGER

from the Hotel Queen Mary, Long Beach, California

$1/3$ pound extra-lean ground sirloin
1 sesame seed roll
$1/2$ ounce sliced mushrooms, grilled
3 slices of fresh avocado
$1/2$ ounce white onion, grilled
1 ounce Monterey cheese
1 slice ripe tomato

Cook hamburger to desired doneness, place on roll, and garnish with grilled mushrooms, avocado, grilled onion, cheese, and tomato slice.

Yield: 1 hamburger sandwich

Beef makes a double contribution regarding iron. It not only provides this important mineral in a form that is easily used by the body, but it also helps in the absorption of iron from other sources like vegetables and beans.

BURGER ROYALE

from Bally's Park Place Casino-Hotel, Atlantic City, New Jersey

6-ounce hamburger patty
2 ounces smoked Swiss cheese
2 ounces crisp Canadian bacon
Lettuce
Tomato slices
Onion slices
Sesame seed bun

Cook hamburger to desired doneness and top with Swiss cheese, Canadian bacon, lettuce, tomato, and onion. Serve on a sesame seed bun.

Yield: 1 hamburger sandwich

Customers who come for dinner at Clint Eastwood's Hog's Breath Inn in Carmel-by-the-Sea, California (where the movie star is also the mayor), can enjoy the Dirty Harry Burger, a cooked patty of ground chuck topped with sautéed mushrooms.

DR. JOYCE BROTHERS'S MEAT LOAF

2 cups fresh bread crumbs
3/4 cup minced onion
1/4 cup minced green pepper
2 eggs
2 pounds chuck, ground
2 tablespoons horseradish
2 1/2 teaspoons salt
1 teaspoon dry mustard
1/4 cup milk or evaporated milk
3/4 cup ketchup

1. When it's convenient, prepare bread crumbs, minced onion, green pepper.

2. About 1 hour before serving: Start heating oven to 400° F.

3. In a large bowl, with fork, beat eggs slightly. Lightly mix in chuck, then crumbs, onion, pepper. (Meat will be juicier and more tender if you handle it as little as possible.) Add horseradish, salt, mustard, milk, 1/4 cup ketchup; combine lightly but well.

4. In bowl, shape meat into oval loaf; transfer to shallow baking dish or broil-and-serve platter; smooth into shapely loaf. Spread top with 1/2 cup ketchup. Bake 50 minutes.

5. Serve from baking dish or broil-and-serve platter, pouring off excess juices. Or, with 2 broad spatulas, lift loaf out of baking dish onto heated platter. Spoon some of the juices over meat. (Nice chilled, then served sliced, too.)

Yield: 8 servings

P. S. If you prefer a soft, moist exterior, bake meat loaf as directed, in 9″ × 5″ × 3″ loaf pan. Pour juices from pan after baking. Unmold meat loaf onto cake rack; then place, right side up, on heated platter.

On one episode of the *Cosby Show* on NBC television, Bill Cosby's son, Theo, played by actor Malcolm-Jamal Warner, called attractive girls "burgers" and very attractive girls "deluxe burgers."

DOM DELUISE'S MEATBALLS

2 pounds ground chuck
1/2 pound ground pork
2 cups Italian-flavored bread crumbs
4 eggs
1 cup milk
1 cup chopped fresh parsley
1/2 cup grated Parmesan cheese
1 tablespoon olive oil (plus additional oil for frying)
2 garlic cloves, chopped very fine
1 onion, minced
1/2 cup pinole (pine nuts)

BILLIE JEAN
KING'S FAVORITE
HAMBURGER
"I grew up in Cali-
fornia. I'll go with
the good old Cali-
fornia burger—
lettuce, tomato,
and lots of mayo."

Place all ingredients in a large bowl and mix thoroughly. Let stand one-half hour. Shape into meatballs. Fry gently in olive oil, or place meatballs on tin foil on a cookie sheet and bake for 1/2 hour at 350° F. Gently place meatballs in your own hot spaghetti sauce and cook on medium-low heat for 1 hour.

Yield: 8 servings

THE TRUFFLE SHALLOT BURGER

from The Ritz-Carlton, Boston, Massachusetts

6 ounces fresh ground sirloin
2 teaspoons minced shallots sautéed in 1 teaspoon butter
*   until tender*
1 teaspoon chopped black truffle
1 teaspoon truffle juice
1/2 teaspoon fresh thyme

Mix all ingredients and form into a patty 1″ thick. Broil or sauté until medium rare. Place on a toasted sourdough bulkie roll and top with 2 ounces havarti cheese.

Serve with deep-fried red-skin potato wedges (3 ounces), tomato slices (1 ounce), lettuce (1 leaf). Garnish with a large sprig of watercress and several cornichons (1 ounce).

Yield: 1 hamburger sandwich

McDonald's opened a restaurant in Water Tower Place, a plush shopping center in Chicago with upscale trappings including $200,000 condominiums, the Ritz Carlton Hotel, and a Halston boutique.

Within hours after the restaurant opened, fur-draped shoppers were waiting in line to be served, and less than nine months later the restaurant was so busy that it was expanded to twice its original size.

SUPERLATIVE HAMBURGER SAUCE DIANE

from The Ponchartrain Hotel, New Orleans, Louisiana

2 pounds ground chuck

Grill patties (6–8 ounces each).

SAUCE DIANE

1 bunch green onions
5 ounces A.1. Steak Sauce
5 ounces Lea & Perrins Worcestershire Sauce
1 pint beef stock (or 1 can beef broth)

Chop onions and mix with other ingredients. Simmer until thickened.

Spread generously over grilled burgers.

Yield: 4 to 5 burgers

For most people, a trip to a fast-food restaurant is a routine, unnoticed activity. But when a former President of the United States does it, it is big enough news for the Associated Press wire service to carry the story.

According to John Taylor, a spokesman for former President Richard Nixon who was quoted in the AP dispatch, the weather was nice on Wednesday, April 2, 1986, so Mr. Nixon decided to leave his home in Saddle River in northern New Jersey and go for a

HERITAGE "MAYTAG BLUE" BURGER

from The Heritage, Cincinnati, Ohio

30 ounces ground sirloin (85% lean, 15% fat)
6 ounces Maytag blue cheese
6 tablespoons sweet butter, softened
1 tablespoon Lea & Perrins Worcestershire sauce
1¹/₂ tablespoons fresh garlic chives
White pepper to taste
6 slices beefsteak tomato
6 slices Vidalia onion in season (or Bermuda onion)
6 poppy-seed Kaiser rolls, split and grilled

Grind sirloin and fat to 85% lean, 15% fat on ³/₈ inch grind. Refrigerate for later use.

Combine Maytag blue cheese (crumbled), Worcestershire sauce, butter, fresh garlic chives, and white pepper, and work into a paste. Refrigerate.

Scale ground sirloin into 5-ounce patties. Make a well in the center of each patty, and fill with 1¹/₂ ounces of blue cheese mixture. Slightly flatten the patty, working the ground sirloin over the well. The blue cheese mixture should be completely encased.

Mesquite grill the burger to desired doneness. Top with beefsteak tomato and Vidalia onion. Serve on toasted, buttered Kaiser roll.

Yield: 6 hamburger sandwiches

drive along the Jersey shore and have a hamburger and some french fries.

Along with a member of his staff, President Nixon stopped for lunch at 12:30 P.M. at the Burger King on Route 72 in the town of Stafford in Ocean County.

Besides eating his lunch, the former President signed autographs, posed for pictures, and left a note reading:

Best Wishes to Burger King, home of the Whopper. Love, Richard Nixon.

19

THE BEST
BEEF
BURGERS

ROQUEFORT AND WINE BURGERS

2 pounds ground beef
6 tablespoons chopped shallots
6 tablespoons chopped parsley
Salt to taste
1/4 teaspoon pepper
1/4 teaspoon paprika
6 fresh mushrooms, chopped
6 tablespoons red wine
6 tablespoons crumbled Roquefort cheese

Combine meat, shallots, parsley, salt, pepper, paprika, and mushrooms. Shape into 6 patties.

Form an indentation in the top of each patty. Place patties in a shallow pan, pour wine over patties, and chill in refrigerator for 2 to 4 hours.

Broil.

Just before serving, remove hamburgers from broiler, place 1 tablespoon of Roquefort cheese in the indentation in each hamburger, and broil until cheese melts.

Yield: 6 burgers

Hamburger has its origins in the steak tartare—shredded raw meat seasoned with salt, pepper, and onion juice—eaten by people in the Baltic provinces of Russia. They were introduced to this dish by the Tartars, who were originally a nomadic tribe from eastern Central Asia.

23

COLBY AND ONION BURGER

6 tablespoons chopped onion
1 1/2 teaspoons butter or margarine
2 pounds ground beef
1/2 teaspoon celery salt
Dash pepper
1 tablespoon ketchup
3 ounces Colby cheese, cut into 6 equal slices

Sauté onion in butter until golden brown.

Combine sautéed onion, meat, celery salt, pepper, and ketchup. Shape into 12 thin patties.

Place the Colby cheese slices on top of 6 of the patties. Cover with remaining patties, gently pressing together edges of patties to seal cheese inside.

Pan-fry in the same pan used to fry onions.

Yield: 6 burgers

PHILADELPHIA,
PENNSYLVANIA
At Bookbinder's, a
Chopped Sirloiner
costs $16.25 and
comes with a green
vegetable and
either french fries
or a baked potato.

HOT CHILI CON CARNE BURGERS

1 1/2 cups chopped onion
1/2 cup chopped green pepper
1/2 cup chopped red pepper
1 1/2 tablespoons cooking oil
2 pounds ground beef
1/4 teaspoon pepper
1 1/2 teaspoons dried oregano
1 teaspoon ground cumin
1 tablespoon crushed garlic clove
2 tablespoons chili powder
2 cups tomato sauce
1 tablespoon wine vinegar
1/4 teaspoon hot pepper flakes

BALTIMORE, MARYLAND Gordon's has an inexpensive basic burger for $2.50.

Sauté onion, green pepper, and red pepper in cooking oil, cooking until onion is soft and transparent.

Combine sautéed onion and peppers, meat, pepper, oregano, cumin, garlic, and chili powder, mixing thoroughly. Shape into 6 patties.

Broil.

Combine tomato sauce, vinegar, and hot pepper flakes. Baste hamburgers several times with mixture while broiling.

Yield: 6 burgers

SWEET PICKLE HAMBURGER

2 pounds ground beef
1 cup chopped sweet pickles
3 small scallions, chopped
Salt to taste
1/4 teaspoon pepper
Ketchup

Combine meat, pickles, scallions, salt, and pepper. Shape into 6 patties.

Broil, remove from oven, top patties with ketchup, and return to broiler for an additional minute or two.

Yield: 6 burgers

During the early 1930s, British Professor Ronald Elwy Mitchell spent three years in the United States studying America and Americans.

He then wrote a guide book *(America: A Practical Handbook)* to explain this country to his fellow Englishmen and, as Professor Mitchell put it, to "... help in my small way to foster friendly

PIZZA BURGERS

2 pounds ground beef
Salt to taste
1 teaspoon onion powder
1 teaspoon dried oregano
1 cup tomato sauce
¹/₂ cup sliced fresh mushrooms
1 cup shredded mozzarella cheese

Combine meat, salt, onion powder, oregano, and 3 tablespoons of the tomato sauce. Shape into 6 patties.

Broil hamburgers until nearly done. Top with mushrooms, cheese, and remaining tomato sauce. Broil for another 2 to 3 minutes, until cheese melts.

Yield: 6 burgers

relations between two great English-speaking nations."

In describing the great size and diversity of the United States, Professor Mitchell noted that America is ". . . a country where you can drive the distance from Calais to Constantinople or from Malaga to Moscow and be understood when you ask for a hamburger sand-wich or pie à la mode."

GRILLED PARMESAN BURGERS

2 pounds ground beef
Salt to taste
$^1/_2$ teaspoon pepper
1$^1/_2$ cups chopped onion
2 tablespoons chopped fresh parsley
3 eggs
$^2/_3$ cup grated Parmesan cheese
$^1/_2$ teaspoon Tabasco sauce
3 cups bread crumbs
2 tablespoons olive oil

Combine meat, salt, pepper, onion, parsley, eggs, Parmesan cheese, and Tabasco sauce. Shape into 6 patties.

Coat patties with bread crumbs and pan-fry in olive oil.

Yield: 6 burgers

German immigrants who came to the United States in the late 1800s on the ships of the Hamburg-Amerika Line were served patties of dried beef, bread crumbs, and onion.

HAMBURGER EGG SURPRISE

2 pounds ground beef
2 tablespoons sweet relish
1 teaspoon celery salt
$^1/_4$ teaspoon pepper
$1^1/_2$ teaspoons prepared mustard
1 hard-boiled egg

On average, each person in the United States eats three hamburgers a week for a total consumption in the country of about 38 billion hamburgers a year.

Combine meat, relish, celery salt, pepper, and mustard. Shape into 12 thin patties.

Cut hard-boiled egg into 6 slices and place slices on top of 6 of the patties. Cover with remaining patties, gently pressing together edges of patties to seal egg inside.

Pan-fry.

Yield: 6 burgers

SNAPPYBURGERS

2 pounds ground beef
6 tablespoons grated onion
Salt to taste
Dash pepper
1/4 cup bread crumbs
1 egg
3/4 teaspoon celery seed

TOMATO AND GINGER SAUCE

8 ounces tomato sauce
1/2 cup water
1/4 cup vinegar
1/4 cup brown sugar
6 gingersnaps, broken into small pieces
6 whole cloves
1 bay leaf

Combine meat, onion, salt, pepper, bread crumbs, egg, and celery seed. Shape into 6 patties.

Pan-fry until brown on both sides.

Combine sauce ingredients and pour over hamburgers. Simmer loosely covered for 45 minutes. Remove bay leaf from sauce before serving.

Yield: 6 burgers

The place was St. Louis, Missouri. The year was 1904. The song was "Meet Me in St. Louis, Louis." The event was the Louisiana Purchase Exposition—World's Fair, a celebration of the one hundredth anniversary of the Louisiana Purchase, which doubled the size of the United States.

The Exposition, which included the 1904 Olympic Games, was one of the greatest shows of its time. More than 20 million people viewed thousands of exhibits from 45 states and 35 countries. The exhibits included the Liberty Bell on its first trip west of the Mississippi River; over 160

BAKED BEER BURGERS

2 pounds ground beef
Dash pepper
1 teaspoon Tabasco sauce
1 garlic clove, crushed
1/3 cup chili sauce
1/2 package dry onion soup mix
1/2 cup beer

Preheat oven to 400° F.

Combine meat, pepper, Tabasco sauce, garlic, chili sauce, dry onion soup mix, and 1/4 cup of the beer. Shape into 6 patties.

Bake at 400° F until brown, about 10 minutes. Baste with remaining 1/4 cup of the beer.

Continue baking for an additional 10 to 15 minutes, until done.

Yield: 6 burgers

automobiles powered by petroleum, electricity, and steam; the giant Floral Clock, 112 feet in diameter and with hands weighing 2,500 pounds; and the Observation Wheel, a 250-foot-tall Ferris wheel that could hold 2,000 people and that made one complete turn every 15 minutes.

In addition to these spectacular exhibits, there were two equally spectacular culinary firsts. Ice cream cones were invented and first served at the fair, and the American people were introduced to the hamburger sandwich, a cooked patty of chopped meat served on a bun.

HAMBURGERS EN CROÛTE

2 pounds ground beef
Salt to taste
1 tablespoon butter or margarine
2 8-ounce packages refrigerator biscuits
2 tablespoons prepared mustard
1/4 pound liverwurst
1/4 cup sliced fresh mushrooms

Preheat oven to 450° F.

Shape ground beef into 6 patties and sprinkle with salt.

Brown patties in butter on both sides. Remove from pan and place on paper towels. Set aside.

On floured surface and using floured rolling pin, roll biscuit dough into 12 4-inch diameter circles.

Spread mustard on dough circles and place patties on top. Evenly spread liverwurst and then mushrooms on top of patties.

Cover with remaining dough circles, firmly pressing edges together to seal hamburgers inside.

Place patties on lightly greased cookie sheet and bake at 450° F for about 20 minutes, until crust is golden brown.

Yield: 6 hamburger pies

The first McDonald's fast-food restaurant opened on April 15, 1955, at 400 North Lee Street in Des Plaines, Illinois. The full name of the restaurant was McDonald's Spee-dee Service Drive-In.

By the end of 1985, there were nearly 9,000 McDonald's restaurants in the United States and 34 foreign countries.

About 500 new McDonald's are opened each year—about one every 17 hours.

CORDON BLEU HAMBURGERS

1/2 cup bread crumbs
1/4 cup milk
2 pounds ground beef
1/4 teaspoon pepper
1/2 teaspoon celery salt
1 egg
6 slices ham
6 slices Swiss cheese

Soak bread crumbs in milk until softened.

Combine softened bread crumbs, meat, pepper, celery salt, and egg. Shape into 12 thin patties.

Place 1 slice of ham and 1 slice of cheese on top of each of 6 of the patties. Cover with remaining patties, gently pressing together edges of patties to seal ham and cheese inside.

Broil.

Yield: 6 burgers

More ground beef is sold in the United States than any other kind of meat.

BARBECUE BURGERS

2 pounds ground beef
1 egg
1 onion, chopped
1/2 cup cracker crumbs
1/4 cup ketchup
2 tablespoons brown sugar
3 teaspoons prepared mustard
Barbecue Burger Sauce (recipe follows)

Combine meat, egg, onion, cracker crumbs, ketchup, sugar, and mustard. Shape into 6 patties.

Grill, brushing frequently with Barbecue Burger Sauce.

Yield: 6 burgers

By 1932, about four years after the White Castle hamburger chain started in business, the name "hamburger stand" was in common use.

BARBECUE BURGER SAUCE

1 garlic clove, crushed
1/4 cup chopped onion
1 1/2 teaspoons cooking oil
1/4 cup tomato paste
1/4 cup chili sauce
1/4 cup wine vinegar
2 tablespoons ginger ale
1 tablespoon sugar
Salt to taste
1/4 teaspoon pepper
1/2 teaspoon ground allspice
1/4 teaspoon ground mace
1/2 teaspoon Tabasco sauce

Sauté garlic and onion in oil until onion becomes soft and transparent. Add tomato paste, chili sauce, vinegar, ginger ale, sugar, salt, pepper, allspice, mace, and Tabasco sauce.

Simmer, uncovered, for about 15 minutes.

Yield: Approximately 1 cup

CURRIED OAT HAMBURGERS

2 pounds ground beef
Salt to taste
¹/8 teaspoon pepper
³/4 cup quick oats
¹/3 cup finely chopped celery
¹/4 cup grated carrot
¹/3 cup finely chopped onion
2 tablespoons chopped fresh parsley
¹/2 teaspoon dried oregano
1 teaspoon curry powder
1 egg, lightly beaten
6 tablespoons tomato juice

Combine all ingredients. Shape into 6 patties.
Broil.

Yield: 6 burgers

NEW YORK, N. Y.
At Hamburger
Harry's, a basic
cheeseburger costs
$4.25. For $6.25
you can get a
deluxe model with
caviar and sour
cream.

ONION SURPRISE HAMBURGERS

2 pounds ground beef
Salt to taste
Dash pepper
2 eggs
¹/₂ cup bread crumbs
1 envelope dry onion soup mix stirred with 3 tablespoons
    water

Combine meat, salt, pepper, eggs, and bread crumbs. Shape into 12 thin patties.

Spoon equal amounts of onion soup mixture onto 6 of the patties. Cover with remaining patties, gently pressing together edges of patties to seal onion soup filling inside.

Grill or pan-fry.

Yield: 6 burgers

WASHINGTON, D. C.
The Georgetown Bar & Grill has a burger with french fries for $6.95.

CHILI CHEESEBURGERS

2 pounds ground beef
Salt to taste
Dash pepper
1 garlic clove, crushed
³/4 cup shredded Monterey Jack cheese
1 16-ounce can chili with beans
Lettuce
Onion slices

Hamburgers have become so much a part of the American diet, and they are eaten so frequently, that a young mother in the Midwest, who has remained anonymous, described hamburgers as "The Daily Grind."

Combine meat, salt, pepper, garlic, cheese, and chili. Shape into 6 patties.
Broil.
Serve garnished with lettuce and onions.

Yield: 6 burgers

CARAWAY BURGERS

1 large slice rye bread
1/4 cup milk
2 pounds ground beef
3/4 teaspoon caraway seeds
1/2 teaspoon dried tarragon
1/4 teaspoon celery seeds
1 egg, lightly beaten
2 tablespoons cooking oil

Soak rye bread in milk until soggy and then mash.

Combine mashed bread, meat, caraway seeds, tarragon, celery seeds, and egg. Mix well. Shape into 6 patties.

Pan-fry in oil.

Yield: 6 burgers

Around 1940, hamburgers replaced hot dogs as the most popular quick food in the United States.

BURGERS ITALIANO

RICHMOND,
VIRGINIA
Lightfoot's Lounge
at the Hyatt Rich-
mond has a burger
called the Ameri-
can Legend. It
comes with cole-
slaw and costs
$6.50, and they'll
add free of charge
all kinds of
goodies, including
guacamole, mush-
rooms, and danish
bleu cheese.

2 pounds ground beef
Salt to taste
Dash pepper
1/2 teaspoon dried oregano
2 tablespoons chopped fresh parsley
2 garlic cloves, crushed
1 anchovy, mashed
1/4 cup bread crumbs
1/4 teaspoon grated lemon peel
1 egg
3 to 4 tablespoons olive oil

Combine meat, salt, pepper, oregano, parsley, garlic, anchovy, bread crumbs, lemon peel, and egg. Shape into 6 patties.

Pan-fry hamburgers in heated olive oil.

Yield: 6 burgers

WESTERN HAMBURGERS

2 pounds ground beef
Salt to taste
2 tablespoons chopped fresh parsley
1 1/2 cups chopped onion
2 eggs
2 tablespoons chopped green chili peppers
1 teaspoon dried oregano
1/4 teaspoon ground cumin
Ranch Sauce (recipe follows)

Combine meat, salt, parsley, onion, eggs, chili peppers, oregano, and cumin. Shape into 6 patties.
Broil.
Serve with Ranch Sauce.

Yield: 6 burgers

RANCH SAUCE

2 tablespoons cooking oil
3 large tomatoes, crushed
1 onion, finely chopped
Dash salt
1 teaspoon sugar
1 tablespoon vinegar
1/4 teaspoon hot pepper flakes
1 1/2 tablespoons chopped green chili peppers
1 green pepper, finely chopped

Heat oil in a saucepan. Add tomatoes and onion, cooking for about 20 to 25 minutes, until mixture is thick. Stir in salt, sugar, vinegar, hot pepper flakes, chili peppers, and green pepper.
Simmer, uncovered, for 10 minutes.

Yield: Approximately 3 cups

Hamburgers get their name from the port city of Hamburg in northern Germany, where the people took the steak tartare from the Russian Baltic provinces, shaped the meat into patties, and then cooked them. The new dish was called Hamburg steak.

Sauerbraten Burgers

2 pounds ground beef
2 tablespoons grated onion
Salt to taste
1/4 teaspoon pepper
1/4 cup bread crumbs
1/3 cup light cream
1 teaspoon grated lemon peel
1 tablespoon butter or margarine

Sweet and Sour Ginger Sauce
1 *1/4* cups beef consommé
1/8 teaspoon ground cloves
3 tablespoons wine vinegar
1/2 teaspoon ground ginger
1/4 cup brown sugar
1/4 cup raisins

Combine meat, onion, salt, pepper, bread crumbs, light cream, and lemon peel. Shape into 6 patties. Set aside.

Combine all the sauce ingredients in a frying pan and heat to boiling. Decrease heat and simmer for about 5 minutes.

Pan-fry patties in melted butter in second frying pan on both sides. Pour hot Sweet and Sour Ginger Sauce over patties in frying pan, cover, and cook about 10 minutes, until done.

Yield: 6 burgers

Nine out of ten households in the United States serve hamburgers at least once every two weeks.

STUFFED BACON-CHEESEBURGERS

2 pounds ground beef
Salt to taste
$1/4$ teaspoon pepper
2 tablespoons barbecue sauce
$1^1/2$ teaspoons sesame seeds
3 strips cooked bacon, crumbled
1 teaspoon cooking oil
6 ounces Cheddar cheese

The name "cheese-burger" was first used during the 1930s.

Combine ground beef, salt, pepper, barbecue sauce, and sesame seeds. Shape into 12 thin patties.

Evenly sprinkle bacon over tops of 6 of the patties. Cover with remaining patties, gently pressing together edges of patties to seal bacon inside.

Pan-fry in oil until almost done. Place Cheddar cheese on top of hamburgers, cover, and cook until cheese melts.

Yield: 6 burgers

ORIENTAL BURGERS

CHARLOTTE,
NORTH
CAROLINA
The Hereford Barn
Steak House has a
children's burger
for only $2.75,
including salad,
french fries, onion
rings, and a coke.

2 pounds ground beef
1/4 teaspoon pepper
1/4 cup cold water
1 garlic clove, crushed
1 tablespoon cooking oil
1/8 teaspoon ground ginger
3 tablespoons soy sauce
3/4 cup water chestnuts, thinly sliced
1 tablespoon honey

Combine meat, pepper, water, and garlic. Shape into 6 patties.

Brown hamburgers in heated oil in frying pan, 3 minutes on each side.

Combine ginger, soy sauce, water chestnuts, and honey.

Pour ginger mixture over hamburgers in pan and cook over low heat for about 5 minutes, turning often.

Yield: 6 burgers

Scallion Butter Burgers

2 pounds ground beef
Salt to taste
1/4 teaspoon celery seed
1/2 cup chopped scallions
3/4 teaspoon coarsely ground black pepper
Scallion Butter (recipe follows)
12 slices rye bread

Combine meat, salt, celery seed, and scallions. Shape into 6 patties. Press pepper into surface of patties.
Grill.
Toast rye bread and spread with Scallion Butter. Place hamburgers on toasted rye bread.

Yield: 6 burgers

Scallion Butter

2 tablespoons finely chopped scallion greens
4 tablespoons butter or margarine, softened
1 garlic clove, crushed
1 tablespoon chopped fresh parsley
1 tablespoon lemon juice

Combine all ingredients, blending well.

From November 11, 1985, until 150 days, 1 hour, 6 minutes, and 26,280 miles later on April 11, 1986, Dodge Morgan singlehandedly sailed his sixty-foot cutter, *American Promise,* around the world and set a new record for solo, nonstop circumnavigation of the earth.

During the entire trip he took on board no extra food in addition to what he had when

HEALTHY HAMBURGERS

2 pounds ground beef
2 eggs
¹/4 cup chopped green pepper
1 tomato, chopped
¹/4 cup chopped green olives stuffed with pimiento
1 onion, finely chopped
¹/2 cup grated Cheddar cheese
3 tablespoons wheat germ
¹/4 cup chopped walnuts

Combine all the ingredients. Shape into 6 patties. Broil.

Yield: 6 burgers

he started, received no assistance from any other boat, and never used the motor for propulsion.

Upon arriving back at his starting point in St. George, Bermuda, Morgan was rewarded with a ceremonial cheeseburger, his favorite meal, served on a silver platter by David Hillier, the owner of the nearby White Horse Tavern.

SLOPPY JOES

³/4 cup finely chopped onion
¹/2 cup chopped green pepper
¹/2 cup chopped mushrooms
2 tablespoons butter or margarine
2 pounds ground beef
1¹/2 teaspoons chili powder
Dash red pepper
1 cup tomato sauce
6 hamburger rolls

In a large pan, sauté onions, green pepper, and mushrooms in butter, cooking until onions become soft and transparent.

Add meat, chili powder, red pepper, and tomato sauce to pan, mixing well. Simmer until meat is thoroughly cooked.

Spoon over open hamburger rolls.

Yield: 6 sloppy joes

The five largest fast-food chains specializing in hamburgers are, in rank order:

1. McDonald's
2. Burger King
3. Wendy's
4. Hardee's
5. Jack in the Box

TACO PITA POCKETS

2 pounds ground beef
Salt to taste
Dash pepper
1/2 teaspoon celery seed
2 tablespoons prepared mustard
2 tablespoons Worcestershire sauce
1 egg
3/4 cup crushed taco-flavored tortilla chips
6 slices cheese
6 slices tomato
6 slices onion
3 large pickles, thinly sliced
4 tablespoons butter or margarine, melted
10 drops Tabasco sauce
6 pita pockets
Lettuce
Tomato
Onion

Combine meat, salt, pepper, celery seed, mustard, Worcestershire sauce, egg, and tortilla chips. Shape into 2 large thin patties, about 5 inches in diameter.

On one of the patties, arrange 3 slices of the cheese, 6 tomato slices, 6 onion slices, and all the pickle slices. Top with remaining 3 slices of cheese.

Cover with the other patty and gently press together the edges to seal the filling inside.

Broil.

Combine butter and Tabasco sauce and baste hamburger when almost done.

Cut hamburger into 6 wedges and place in pita pockets. Garnish with lettuce, tomato, and onion.

Yield: 6 hamburger sandwiches

In the late 1940s, hamburgers became even more popular in America because of three reasons: the end of World War II meant more meat was available, life-styles were more informal, and backyard cookouts were popular.

Although the population of Europe is nearly three times as great as the population of the United States, more ground beef is eaten in America than in all the countries of Europe combined.

NUTTY BURGERS

2 pounds ground beef
Salt to taste
Dash pepper
1/2 teaspoon celery seed
1 shallot, finely chopped
1 garlic clove, crushed
1 tablespoon chopped fresh parsley
1 1/2 teaspoons bread crumbs
1 tablespoon grated Parmesan or Romano cheese
1/2 cup chopped almonds or pine nuts
2 eggs
1/4 cup oil and vinegar or Italian salad dressing

Combine meat, salt, pepper, celery seed, shallot, garlic, parsley, bread crumbs, cheese, nuts, and eggs. Shape into 6 patties.

Broil, basting with salad dressing.

Yield: 6 burgers

Ronald McDonald made his first public appearance in 1963 in Washington, D. C. He was played by Willard Scott, who is now the weatherman on the *Today* show on NBC.

BEEFBURGER REUBEN

2 pounds ground beef
1 slice bread, broken into very small pieces
Salt to taste
$1/4$ teaspoon pepper
6 slices rye bread
$1 1/4$ cups Thousand Island Dressing (recipe follows)
6 slices Swiss cheese
8 ounces sauerkraut, drained
2 tablespoons butter or margarine

Mix together meat, bread pieces, salt, and pepper. Shape into 6 patties.

Pan-fry.

Remove cooked patties from pan. Place each on a slice of rye bread, top with Thousand Island Dressing, a slice of cheese, and sauerkraut.

Melt butter in pan, place open-faced sandwich in pan, cover, and cook until cheese has melted and rye bread is golden brown.

Yield: 6 hamburger sandwiches

THOUSAND ISLAND DRESSING

1 cup mayonnaise
1 tablespoon ketchup
2 tablespoons finely chopped green pepper
2 tablespoons finely chopped pimiento
1 teaspoon finely chopped onion
1 hard-boiled egg, chopped
1 teaspoon Worcestershire sauce
4 drops Tabasco sauce

Combine all ingredients, mixing well.

Yield: Approximately 1 1/2 cups

ATLANTA,
GEORGIA
At The Lark and the Dove, a lunchtime burger with french fries costs $5.95.

HOAGIEBURGERS

2 pounds ground beef
1 tablespoon Worcestershire sauce
Salt to taste
1/4 teaspoon pepper
2 cups tomato sauce
3/4 cup chili sauce
1*1/2* teaspoons oregano
1*1/2* teaspoons wine vinegar
6 thin slices onion
6 slices tomato
12 slices dill pickle
6 torpedo rolls

Combine meat, Worcestershire sauce, salt, pepper, 1½ cups of the tomato sauce, chili sauce, oregano, and vinegar. Shape into 6 long patties to fit rolls.
Broil.
Place patties in rolls. Spoon remaining ½ cup tomato sauce over hamburgers, and garnish with onion, tomato, and pickle slices.

Yield: 6 burgers

Dr. Michael W. Pariza, a food microbiologist at the University of Wisconsin, has found that cooked hamburgers yield a substance that inhibits cancer in animals. Mice that received a hamburger extract developed two-thirds fewer tumors than did mice in a control group that did not receive the extract.

Although he pointed out that his research data is preliminary and more tests are needed, Dr. Pariza was quoted in *USA Today,* saying, "People have certainly become concerned about the bad things in food, so they might be reassured to know that there are good things in food."

CRANBERRY-CURRY BURGERS

2 pounds ground beef
¹/2 teaspoon celery salt
Dash pepper
2¹/2 teaspoons curry powder
1¹/2 cups canned crushed pineapple in its own juice
6 ¹/2-inch slices cranberry sauce

Mix together meat, celery salt, pepper, and 1 tea-spoon of the curry powder. Shape into 6 patties.

Broil.

While hamburgers are broiling, combine remaining 1¹/2 teaspoons curry powder and crushed pineapple with juice in a saucepan and heat.

Top each broiled hamburger with a slice of cran-berry sauce and hot curry and pineapple sauce.

Yield: 6 burgers

Hamburgers are also called "Wim-pyburgers," named after Wimpy, the character in the *Popeye* comic strip who liked ham-burgers so much.

BRANDY BURGERS

2 pounds ground beef
Salt to taste
1/4 teaspoon pepper
9 tablespoons chopped chives
3 tablespoons butter or margarine
1/4 cup brandy
3 shallots, chopped
1/2 cup sherry

Mix together meat, salt, pepper, and 6 tablespoons of the chives. Shape into 6 patties.

Melt butter in a pan and fry patties. When hamburgers are almost done cooking, leave in pan, pour brandy over top, and ignite. Let flame for a minute or two, then stir in shallots and remaining 3 tablespoons of chives.

Cook for about 3 to 4 minutes more, stirring constantly, until shallots are tender. Add sherry and continue cooking for another minute.

Remove hamburgers and serve topped with sauce from pan.

Yield: 6 burgers

The largest hamburger ever made, according to the *Guinness Book of World Records,* weighed 4,411.41 pounds and had a surface area of 387.5 square feet. This mammoth burger was made on May 26, 1983, by butchers in Brussels, Belgium, and was cut into 7,440 portions after it was grilled.

Avo-Burger-Cado

1 ripe avocado
2 pounds ground beef
1 teaspoon celery seed
Salt to taste
¹/4 teaspoon pepper

Peel and pit avocado. Cut 6 thin slices from the avocado and set aside. Mash remainder of avocado.

Combine mashed avocado, ground beef, celery seed, salt, and pepper. Shape into 6 patties.

Broil, grill, or pan-fry.

Top each hamburger with a slice of avocado.

Yield: 6 burgers

SPROUT BURGERS IN PITA POCKETS

2 pounds ground beef
1 tablespoon soy sauce
1 garlic clove, crushed
6 tablespoons chopped onion
6 tablespoons chopped bean sprouts
1 teaspoon ketchup
3 pita breads, cut in half and split open
Rice Noodle Sauce (recipe follows)

Combine meat, soy sauce, garlic, onion, bean sprouts, and ketchup. Shape into 6 patties.

Broil, grill, or pan-fry.

Place hamburgers in pita pockets and cover with heated Rice Noodle Sauce.

Yield: 6 hamburger sandwiches

RICE NOODLE SAUCE

1/4 cup soy sauce
6 tablespoons chopped bean sprouts
6 tablespoons crushed Chinese rice noodles

Combine all the ingredients and let stand for 1 hour. Heat sauce thoroughly.

Yield: Approximately 1 cup

There is a university in the United States that has never had a football team play in a bowl game, never has had a basketball team play in the NCAA tournament, and, in all probability, never has had a student complain about the food in the dining hall. Student rooms in the Lodge, the school dormitory, have private baths, telephones, televisions, daily maid

GARNISHED STEAK TARTARE

2 pounds well-trimmed sirloin, freshly ground
Salt to taste
1/4 teaspoon pepper
1/3 cup chopped fresh parsley
3 tablespoons Cognac
6 egg yolks
1 onion, finely chopped
6 anchovies, mashed
12 capers

Combine meat, salt, pepper, parsley, and Cognac. Shape into 6 patties.

Using a teaspoon, make an indentation in the top of each patty. Place an egg yolk in each indentation. Garnish with onion, anchovies, and capers.

Yield: 6 burgers

service, and private patios.

This university is none other than Hamburger University in Oak Brook, Illinois, operated by McDonald's to train franchise managers. In the twenty-five years since it was founded, the school has graduated nearly 30,000 students and every year 3,000 more are awarded a degree in hamburger-ology.

SCANDINAVIAN BURGERS

2 pounds ground beef
1¹/₄ cups cooked mashed potatoes
Salt to taste
¹/₂ teaspoon pepper
¹/₈ teaspoon ground allspice
2 tablespoons capers
1 egg, lightly beaten
6 tablespoons light cream
¹/₄ cup butter or margarine
2 tablespoons chopped fresh dill
6 hamburger buns
6 cooked beets, sliced

One of the things Duke Ellington did during his tour of the Soviet Union was show Russian chefs how to make hamburgers.

Combine beef, potatoes, salt, pepper, allspice, capers, egg, and light cream. Mix together lightly. Shape into 6 patties.

Broil or grill.

Combine butter and dill, spread on hamburger buns, and lightly toast.

Top hamburgers with beet slices and serve on toasted buns.

Yield: 6 hamburger sandwiches

BACON AND MOZZARELLA BURGERS

6 tablespoons chopped onion
1 1/2 teaspoons butter or margarine
2 pounds ground beef
9 slices cooked bacon, crumbled
1/2 cup shredded mozzarella cheese
1/4 teaspoon celery salt
Dash pepper
1 egg, slightly beaten

Sauté onion in butter until golden brown.

Mix together sautéed onion, meat, bacon, cheese, celery salt, pepper, and egg. Shape into 6 patties.

Pan-fry in the same pan used to fry onions.

Yield: 6 burgers

In an article in the *Reader's Digest* titled "Ten Great Myths of Physical Fitness," myth number 9 was "Don't eat before working out."

This myth was dispelled by physiologist Robert M. Otto, director of the Human Performance Laboratory at Adelphi University in Garden City, New York.

According to Otto, "World records have been set by athletes who ate hamburgers and brownies moments before their event."

SPECIALTY
BURGERS

SPICED TURKEYBURGERS

2 pounds ground turkey
$^1/_4$ teaspoon pepper
$^1/_2$ teaspoon ground cinnamon
$^1/_4$ teaspoon ground nutmeg
2 teaspoons dried mint
2 tablespoons lemon juice
1 garlic clove, crushed
6 tablespoons finely chopped onion
6 tablespoons tomato sauce

Combine turkey, pepper, cinnamon, nutmeg, mint, lemon juice, garlic, onion, and 3 tablespoons of the tomato sauce. Shape into 6 patties.

Grill or broil, brushing often with remaining 3 tablespoons tomato sauce.

Yield: 6 burgers

KEY WEST,
FLORIDA
A burger at Papa
Joe's costs $4.25.
That includes 2
cheeses, mush-
rooms, lettuce,
tomato, pickle, and
french fries.

TANGY CHICKENBURGERS

2 pounds ground chicken
1 cup chopped celery
¹/₄ cup finely chopped onion
2 tablespoons Worcestershire sauce
1 teaspoon dried oregano
1 garlic clove, crushed
¹/₃ cup ketchup
6 slices mozzarella cheese

MINNEAPOLIS,
MINNESOTA
A burger with
french fries costs
$2.95 at Eddie
Webster's.

Combine chicken, celery, onion, Worcestershire sauce, oregano, and garlic. Shape into 6 patties.

Grill or broil, brushing often with ketchup.

Just before burgers are done, top with cheese and continue cooking, covered, until cheese melts.

Yield: 6 burgers

MARINATED VEAL BURGER SANDWICHES

1 pound ground beef
1 pound ground veal
Salt to taste
1 teaspoon pepper
1 teaspoon celery seed
1 garlic clove, crushed
¹/₂ cup ketchup
2 tablespoons chopped onion
6 slices onion
¹/₂ cup wine vinegar
¹/₄ cup cooking oil
¹/₂ teaspoon dried dill weed
12 slices rye bread

Combine meats, salt, pepper, celery seed, garlic, ketchup, and chopped onion. Shape into 12 thin patties.

Wrap patties in wax paper and chill in the refrigerator for 30 to 45 minutes.

Combine slices of onion, cooking oil, and dill weed. Wrap in plastic wrap and chill in refrigerator for 30 to 45 minutes.

Drain onions and save marinade.

Grill hamburgers until done, brushing frequently with marinade.

Toast rye bread and make a sandwich with two patties, a slice of onion in between, and two slices of toasted rye bread.

Yield: 6 hamburger sandwiches

A study conducted at Colorado State University determined that hamburgers are subject to a total of 41,000 various federal and state regulations, many of them based upon 200 laws and 111,000 court cases that established legal precedents.

These rules cover everything in the production and serving of hamburgers, including grazing of the cattle, inspections of the meat, methods of processing, and sanitary conditions in supermarkets and restaurants.

NOODLEBURGERS

1¹/₂ pounds ground beef
¹/₂ pound ground pork
Salt to taste
¹/₄ teaspoon pepper
¹/₂ teaspoon dried sage
¹/₄ cup chopped red and green pepper
1 3-ounce can rice noodles, crushed
1 egg
¹/₂ cup chopped onion
¹/₄ cup tomato sauce

Combine all ingredients. Shape into 6 patties. Pan fry or broil.

Yield: 6 burgers

BEEF AND LIVER BURGERS

1 1/2 pounds ground beef
1/2 pound ground beef liver
1/2 teaspoon ground allspice
1 teaspoon dry mustard
3 tablespoons tomato sauce
2 large onions, thinly sliced
2 tablespoons butter or margarine

Combine meats, allspice, mustard, and tomato sauce. Shape into 6 patties. Set aside.

Sauté onions in butter until soft and transparent. Remove from pan and set aside.

Using the same pan that was used to sauté the onions, brown the patties on both sides. Cover the pan and cook hamburgers until almost done. Add onions and cook for 1 or 2 minutes more.

Serve hamburgers topped with sautéed onions.

Yield: 6 burgers

HOT DOG BURGERS

2 pounds ground beef
Salt to taste
Dash pepper
1 egg
1/4 cup bread crumbs
2 tablespoons tomato sauce
1 tablespoon chopped fresh parsley
3 tablespoons finely chopped onion
3 hot dogs, each cut into 10 slices

Combine ground beef, salt, pepper, egg, bread crumbs, tomato sauce, parsley, and onions. Shape into 6 patties.

Broil patties on one side and turn over. Place 5 hot dog slices on each patty and broil on second side until done.

Yield: 6 burgers

Clara Peller's question, "Where's the beef?", in advertisements for Wendy's hamburgers became so popular that even Walter Mondale used it as a campaign slogan during the Presidential campaign in 1984.

FISHBURGERS

2 15-ounce cans salmon, drained, or 2 12^1/$_2$-ounce cans
  tuna, drained
^{1}/$_4$ teaspoon pepper
1 cup chopped onion
^{1}/$_2$ cup bread crumbs
^{1}/$_2$ cup chopped green and red pepper
2 eggs
2 tablespoons lemon juice
1 teaspoon grated lemon peel
^{3}/$_4$ teaspoon crushed dried rosemary
2 tablespoons cooking oil

Combine salmon or tuna, pepper, onion, bread crumbs, green and red pepper, eggs, lemon juice, lemon peel, and rosemary. Shape into 6 patties.

Pan-fry patties in cooking oil over medium-low heat until golden brown on both sides.

Yield: 6 burgers

There is a major trend in restaurants now to offer upscale gourmet hamburgers. These are thick, plump hamburgers that are made from fresh beef that is cut and ground right on the premises, cooked to order, and served on rolls that are freshly baked right in the restaurant. In addition, an assortment of cheeses and other toppings can be added by the customer.

According to some analysts in the restaurant industry, there could be as many as 3,000 gourmet burger restaurants throughout the United States doing between $2 billion and $3 billion worth of business a year.

VEGGIEBURGERS

2 10^{1}/$_{2}$-ounce cans chick-peas, drained and mashed
1^{1}/$_{2}$ cups finely chopped pecans
1^{1}/$_{2}$ cups whole-wheat bread crumbs
1^{1}/$_{4}$ cups finely chopped spinach
^{3}/$_{4}$ cup grated carrot
^{1}/$_{4}$ cup chopped green and red pepper
6 shallots, chopped
2 tablespoons chopped celery
1 tablespoon chopped fresh parsley
^{1}/$_{4}$ teaspoon pepper
^{1}/$_{4}$ cup mayonnaise
2 tablespoons butter or margarine

Combine chick-peas, pecans, bread crumbs, spinach, carrot, green and red pepper, shallots, celery, parsley, and mayonnaise. Shape into 6 patties.

Sauté patties in butter, cooking until browned on both sides.

Yield: 6 burgers

The first restaurant in the Washington, D. C., area to prohibit smoking entirely was Upstairs at the Hamlet, the second-floor restaurant of the Hamburger Hamlet in Georgetown.

TOFU BURGERS

1 pound tofu
¹/₄ teaspoon pepper
2 cups mashed potatoes
¹/₃ cup shredded cheddar cheese
6 shallots, chopped
¹/₂ teaspoon dried dill weed
¹/₂ cup bread crumbs
2 tablespoons butter or margarine

Thoroughly drain tofu and pat dry. Chop tofu into small pieces.

Combine tofu, pepper, potatoes, cheese, shallots, and dill weed. Shape into 6 patties. Gently coat patties in bread crumbs.

Melt 1 tablespoon of butter in a pan and cook patties over medium heat for about 5 minutes, until bottoms of patties are browned. Add remaining tablespoon of butter and cook other side of patties for about 5 minutes, until browned.

Yield: 6 burgers

SEATTLE,
WASHINGTON
A basic burger at
Andy's Diner runs
between $3.25
and $3.75.

LAMBURGERS

2 pounds ground lamb
Salt to taste
³/₄ cup bread crumbs softened in 3 tablespoons heavy
  cream
¹/₂ teaspoon dried basil
¹/₄ teaspoon chopped fresh parsley
¹/₈ teaspoon grated lemon peel
¹/₄ teaspoon paprika
¹/₈ teaspoon ground nutmeg

Combine all ingredients. Shape into 6 patties.
Broil or pan-fry.

Yield: 6 burgers

When is a hamburger not a hamburger?

When it is a "steakburger."

In television commercials for A.1. Steak Sauce, Brand & Company, Ltd., of London, the manufacturers of the popular sauce, point out that hamburgers are chopped steak, not chopped ham, so it is entirely appropriate to use A.1. Steak Sauce on hamburgers.

THE
EXTRAS

ROLLS

HAMBURGER BUNS: PLAIN & FANCY

3 1/2–4 cups all-purpose flour
3/4 teaspoon salt
2 tablespoons sugar
2 1/2 tablespoons instant nonfat dry milk powder
1 tablespoon dry yeast
3 tablespoons butter or margarine, softened
1 cup very warm water

NOTE: If desired, buns can be made with a variety of toppings. Just before baking, brush tops of buns with melted butter or margarine and add:

• poppy seeds
• sesame seeds
• shredded cheese
• bacon pieces
• chopped chives
• chopped onion
• celery seed
• caraway seeds

In a large bowl, combine 2 cups of the flour with salt, sugar, milk powder, yeast, and butter. Gradually add water, mixing thoroughly. Add another 1/2 cup of flour, mixing well. Stir rapidly for about 2 minutes, scraping down sides of bowl.

Add remaining flour, a little at a time, until dough becomes stiff.

Remove from bowl, place on a floured surface, and knead until dough becomes smooth and elastic, about 10 minutes.

Place in a greased bowl, turning dough to grease completely. Cover and let rise in a warm place until dough doubles in size, about 45 minutes to 1 hour.

Punch dough down and let sit for another 20 minutes.

Divide dough in half and cut each half into 6 equal pieces. Shape each piece into a smooth ball and place about 2 inches apart on a greased baking sheet. Flatten slightly. Cover and let rise in a warm place for about 1 hour.

Preheat oven to 375° F.

Bake buns for 15 to 20 minutes, until lightly browned.

Yield: 12 hamburger buns

FAMILY FAVORITE ROLLS

1/2 cup milk
3 tablespoons sugar
1 teaspoon salt
3 tablespoons butter or margarine
1 tablespoon dry yeast dissolved in 1 1/2 cups warm water
6–6 1/2 cups all-purpose flour
1 egg mixed with 1 tablespoon water

Heat milk over low heat until small bubbles form around edge of pan. Remove from heat and stir in sugar, salt, and butter. Let cool to lukewarm.

Add dissolved yeast and 3 cups of the flour, beating until smooth. Mix in 2 1/2 cups of the flour. Add remaining flour, a little at a time, until dough becomes stiff.

Place dough on a smooth floured surface and knead for 8 to 10 minutes. Put in a greased bowl, turning dough to grease completely. Cover and let rise in a warm place until dough doubles in size, about 1 hour.

Punch down and divide into 12 equal pieces. Shape into balls and flatten slightly. Let rise for about 1 hour.

Preheat oven to 400° F.

Brush egg and water mixture on top of rolls and bake for 12 to 15 minutes, until golden brown.

Yield: 12 rolls

In the *Dictionary of American Slang*, compiled by Harold Wentworth and Stuart Berg Flexner—a book described as "A landmark in American English lexicography" by the *Journal of American Folklore*—there are four meanings listed for the word "hamburger" in addition to the usual ground meat patty: (1) A badly scarred and often-beaten prize fighter; (2) a bum or tramp, anyone who is down and out; (3) an inferior racing dog, literally one that should be ground up for food; and (4) a mixture of mud and "skin-food" used as a facial in beauty parlors.

PITA BREAD

1½ teaspoons dry yeast
1 tablespoon plus ½ teaspoon sugar
1¼ cups lukewarm water
3 cups all-purpose flour
½ teaspoon salt
2 tablespoons cooking oil

Stir together yeast, the ½ teaspoon sugar, and ¼ cup of the water. Set in a warm place until bubbles appear, about 10 minutes.

In a large bowl, thoroughly mix flour, salt, the 1 tablespoon sugar, remaining 1 cup water, and dissolved yeast. Dough will be slightly sticky.

Knead in bowl for about 10 to 12 minutes, until dough becomes smooth.

Grease top of dough with oil, cover, and leave in a warm place for about 1¼ hours, until dough rises and doubles in size.

Punch dough down, knead for a minute or two, and divide into 12 equal pieces. Shape each piece into a smooth ball, cover, and let stand for about 10 minutes.

Preheat oven to 450° F.

Roll out dough balls into 4-inch rounds. Place rounds on ungreased baking sheets and bake for 8 to 10 minutes.

If desired, place under broiler very briefly for a lightly browned top crust.

Let cool, covered with a towel.

Pita breads will puff up while baking and then collapse when cool, but pocket inside for filling will remain.

Can be stored in freezer.

Yield: 12 pita breads

Salads and Sides

CRISPY POTATO SKINS

6 large baking potatoes
4 tablespoons butter or margarine, melted
Salt to taste
Dash pepper
10 to 20 drops Tabasco sauce

Preheat oven to 450° F.

Bake potatoes for about 1 hour, until they are easily pierced with a fork.

Remove potatoes from oven and increase heat to 475° F.

Remove inside of potatoes from skins, leaving a thin layer of potato attached to skin. Cut skins into strips about 1 inch wide.

Place strips on a baking sheet, skin side down. Combine butter, salt, and pepper. Add Tabasco sauce, 10 drops for mild or 20 drops for spicy, and brush butter mixture onto potato skins.

Bake at 475° F for about 6 to 8 minutes, until potato skins are crisp.

Yield: 6 servings

When Frenchmen Alain Pichavant and Stephane Peyron arrived in Miami Beach in early April 1986, after crossing the Atlantic Ocean on a thirty-one-foot sailboard, they were rewarded with a meal of hamburgers.

The two sailors were making a 5,000-nautical-mile sailboard trip from Senegal in western Africa all the way to New York City for the July Fourth Statue of Liberty Centennial celebration.

HOMEMADE FRENCH-FRIED POTATOES

5 large Idaho potatoes
Cold water
Cooking oil
Salt
Ketchup or vinegar

Peel potatoes and cut into strips. Soak in cold water for about 1 hour.

Drain on paper towels and blot completely dry.

Deep-fry potato strips, a few at a time, in very hot cooking oil until golden brown and crisp.

Drain on paper towels. Sprinkle with salt to taste.

Serve french fries with ketchup or sprinkled with vinegar.

Yield: 6 servings

SAN FRANCISCO, CALIFORNIA
At Chic's Place, that basic burger and fries combo costs $5.95.

HOMEMADE POTATO CHIPS

6 large potatoes
1 teaspoon salt
Cold water
Cooking oil
Salt

ANCHORAGE,
ALASKA
Great Alaska Beef
& Sea has a Super
Hamburger with
french fries and
chili for $5.25.

Peel potatoes and slice very thin. Add 1 teaspoon of salt to cold water and soak potato slices for about 15 minutes.

Drain on paper towels and blot completely dry.

Deep-fry potato slices, a few at a time, in very hot cooking oil until golden brown and crisp.

Drain potato chips on paper towels. Sprinkle with salt to taste.

Chips may be served hot or at room temperature.

Yield: 1 medium bowl of potato chips

NANA'S SPECIAL SOUR CREAM POTATO SALAD

6 large new potatoes
2 onions, finely chopped
1 teaspoon salt
¹/₂ teaspoon pepper
¹/₂ teaspoon celery seed
¹/₂ cup mayonnaise
¹/₂ cup sour cream

Boil potatoes until they can be pierced easily with a fork. Remove potatoes from water and cut into chunks.

While potato chunks are still hot, add onions, salt, pepper, celery seed, mayonnaise, and sour cream. Mix together gently but thoroughly.

Yield: 6 servings

Egg Potato Salad

6 large new potatoes
1 large onion, finely chopped
1 tablespoon butter or margarine
4 hard-boiled eggs, chopped
1 teaspoon salt
¹/₂ teaspoon pepper
³/₄ cup chopped celery
1–1¹/₂ cups mayonnaise
1 tablespoon relish
1¹/₂ tablespoons prepared mustard

Boil potatoes until they can be pierced easily with a fork. Remove potatoes from water, remove skins, and cut into chunks.

Sauté onion in butter until golden brown.

Combine potatoes, onion, eggs, salt, pepper, celery, mayonnaise, relish, and mustard. Mix gently but thoroughly.

Yield: 6 servings

DIANE'S MACARONI SALAD

2 cups cooked macaroni
1 cup chopped carrot
$^1/_2$ cup blanched sliced almonds
$^1/_2$ cup sliced black olives plus 3 tablespoons olive liquid
    from can
6 to 10 tablespoons mayonnaise
Dash salt
$^1/_4$ teaspoon pepper
$^1/_2$ cup chopped celery
$^1/_2$ cup chopped sweet gherkin pickles plus 1 tablespoon
    pickle juice from jar

Combine all ingredients, gently but thoroughly mixing together.

Chill in refrigerator before serving.

Yield: 6 servings

Hamburgers are so much a part of the American scene that in the chapter about picnics and outdoor entertaining in *The Amy Vanderbilt Complete Book of Etiquette: A Guide to Contemporary Living,* hamburgers get special mention, along with cocktails and specialty foods, as something readers might want to take along with them on a picnic.

RICE AND WALNUT SALAD

2 cups rice
2 bay leaves
1 garlic clove, crushed
2 cups cooked peas
¹/₄ cup chopped red pepper
¹/₄ cup chopped green pepper
3 shallots, chopped
2 tablespoons chopped pimiento
15 black olives, pitted and sliced
³/₄ cup chopped walnuts
¹/₂ cup oil and vinegar or Italian salad dressing

Following package instructions, cook rice, adding bay leaves and garlic. When rice has finished cooking, remove bay leaves and discard.

To cooked rice, add peas, red and green peppers, shallots, pimiento, olives, walnuts, and salad dressing, mixing gently but thoroughly.

Cover and chill in refrigerator for 8 hours or overnight before serving.

Yield: 6 servings

CUCUMBER AND ONION SALAD

1/2 cup finely chopped onion
2 cups thinly sliced cucumber
1 large zucchini, cut into thin slices
3 tablespoons wine vinegar
2 teaspoons sugar
2 cups chopped firm tomatoes
2 tablespoons chopped fresh basil or 2 teaspoons dried
1/4 cup olive oil

Combine all ingredients, mixing together thoroughly.

Chill in refrigerator for 8 hours or overnight before serving.

Yield: 6 to 8 servings

McDonald's and Burger King's prices vary around the country. Here's how they run in our hometown of East Windsor, New Jersey. A basic hamburger at McDonald's costs 62¢, and the McDLT with cheese—their most expensive burger—costs $1.69. At Burger King, the basic burger is 65¢, and a Double Whopper will set you back $2.79.

MARGE'S COLE SLAW

1 medium cabbage, cored and shredded
2 large carrots, peeled and shredded
¹/₄ cup vinegar
2 tablespoons sugar
1¹/₄ cups mayonnaise
¹/₂ teaspoon salt
¹/₈ teaspoon pepper

Combine all ingredients, mixing thoroughly.
Chill in refrigerator for 8 hours or overnight before serving.

Yield: 6 to 8 servings

STRING BEAN VINAIGRETTE

2 8-ounce cans string beans, including liquid
2 tablespoons vegetable oil
3 tablespoons olive oil
5 tablespoons cider vinegar
2 tablespoons chopped fresh parsley
1 onion, grated
2 tablespoons chopped pimiento
1 1/2 tablespoons chutney
1/4 teaspoon salt
1/2 teaspoon sugar
2 hard-boiled eggs, chopped

Combine all ingredients, mixing gently but thoroughly.

Chill in refrigerator for 8 hours or overnight before serving.

Yield: 6 servings

On February 8, 1979, in Longview, Washington, Alan Peterson set a record by eating 20³/₄ hamburger sandwiches, each burger weighing 3¹/₂ ounces, in 30 minutes.

THREE-BEAN BACON BAKE

5 strips bacon
¹/₂ cup chopped onion
¹/₂ cup ketchup
¹/₂ cup brown sugar
2 tablespoons vinegar
1 teaspoon prepared mustard
2 teaspoons barbecue sauce
1 16-ounce can kidney beans, drained
1 16-ounce can lima beans, drained
1 16-ounce can pork and beans

Preheat oven to 350° F.

Fry bacon, remove from pan, and drain on paper towels.

Using the same pan, fry onion until golden brown. Add ketchup, sugar, vinegar, mustard, and barbecue sauce. Bring to a boil and pour into a large baking dish.

Crumble bacon into baking dish and add all the beans, mixing thoroughly.

Bake for 35 minutes.

Yield: 6–8 servings

BREW-FRIED ONION RINGS

1½ cups beer
(carbonated or flat, cold or at room temperature)
1½ cups all-purpose flour
3 large Bermuda onions, sliced and separated into rings
Cooking oil

Stir beer gradually into flour, blending gently until smooth. Cover and let batter sit at room temperature for 3 to 4 hours.

Preheat oven to 200° F.

Dip onion rings in batter, coating completely. Fry in hot cooking oil until golden brown.

Drain fried onion rings on paper towels.

Place drained onion rings on a cookie sheet that has been covered with paper towels. Place cookie sheet in preheated oven to keep onion rings warm until serving.

Yield: 6 servings

CHEESE-BRAISED ONIONS

4 large onions, cut into 6 slices each
6 tablespoons butter or margarine
1/4 cup beef gravy
1/4 cup water
1/4 teaspoon salt
Dash pepper
1/4 cup grated Parmesan cheese

Sauté onions in butter, until lightly browned. Add gravy, water, salt, and pepper. Cook until onions become tender, about 20 minutes.

Remove onions from pan, sprinkle with cheese, and broil for 1 to 2 minutes.

Yield: 6 servings

MARINATED MUSHROOMS

1/2 cup water
2/3 cup olive oil
Juice of 2 lemons
1 bay leaf
2 garlic cloves, crushed
6 whole peppercorns
1/4 teaspoon salt
1 pound fresh small mushrooms, washed and trimmed

Combine water, olive oil, lemon juice, bay leaf, garlic, peppercorns, and salt in a pan. Heat to boiling, reduce heat, cover, and then simmer for 15 minutes.

Remove bay leaf and peppercorns by straining and return liquid to pan.

Add mushrooms and simmer for 5 minutes, stirring constantly.

Remove from heat, let cool, and chill in refrigerator in covered container for 8 hours or overnight.

For serving, remove mushrooms from liquid with slotted spoon.

Yield: Approximately 2 cups

There are about 30,000 fast-food restaurants of all kinds in the United States and they sell about $20 billion worth of hamburgers each year.

FRIED MUSHROOMS

²/₃ cup club soda or seltzer
1 cup pancake mix
1 pound fresh mushrooms, washed and trimmed
Cooking oil

Preheat oven to 200° F.

Stir soda gradually into pancake mix, blending gently until smooth.

Dip mushrooms in batter, coating completely. Fry in hot cooking oil until golden brown.

Drain fried mushrooms on paper towels.

Place drained mushrooms on a cookie sheet that has been covered with paper towels. Place cookie sheet in preheated oven to keep mushrooms warm until serving.

Yield: 6 servings

RELISHES AND KETCHUP

MILD TOMATO PEPPER RELISH

2 cups finely chopped tomatoes
1 green pepper, finely chopped
1 red pepper, finely chopped
1 onion, finely chopped
1/2 cup cider vinegar
1 tablespoon sugar
3/4 teaspoon salt
1/2 teaspoon ground cinnamon

In a heavy saucepan, combine all ingredients, mixing thoroughly.

Slowly bring mixture to a boil, reduce heat, and simmer, uncovered, for about 50 minutes to 1 hour, stirring occasionally, until relish thickens.

Chill in refrigerator before serving.

Yield: Approximately 2 cups

CORN RELISH

1 1/2 cups canned corn or fresh or frozen corn, cooked and
   cooled
1/3 cup finely chopped onion
1/3 cup chopped green and red pepper
2 tablespoons vinegar
1 tablespoon vegetable oil
1/3 cup chopped pimiento
2 tablespoons sugar
1 teaspoon dry mustard
Dash salt
Dash pepper

Combine all ingredients, mixing together thoroughly.

Yield: Approximately 2 1/2 cups

During the advertising wars in late 1982 that included claims, counter claims, and lawsuits in federal courts, all three major hamburger fast-food chains—McDonald's, Burger King, and Wendy's—claimed that their hamburgers tasted the best and were the ones preferred by the American people.

The head of Wendy's, Robert L. Barney, challenged his competitors to a national taste test with hamburger eaters to settle the issue, but this important competition never took place.

APPLE APRICOT CHUTNEY

1 apple, peeled, cored, and finely chopped
³/4 cup finely chopped dried apricots
3 tomatoes, finely chopped
¹/2 cup finely chopped red pepper
1 cup finely chopped onion
1 tablespoon crumbled dried mint leaves
1 teaspoon dry mustard
1 teaspoon salt
¹/2 cup brown sugar
1 cup vinegar, boiled and cooled

Combine all ingredients in a heavy saucepan and cook over low heat for about 60 minutes, until mixture becomes very thick.

Store in refrigerator in a tightly covered jar.

Yield: Approximately 2 cups

GOOD AND SPICY KETCHUP

1 onion, cut into chunks
1 garlic clove
5 tablespoons frozen apple juice concentrate
1 6-ounce can tomato paste
1/2 cup cider vinegar
1/4 teaspoon pepper
1/4 teaspoon red pepper flakes
1/4 teaspoon ground cinnamon
1/8 teaspoon ground cloves

Combine onion, garlic clove, and apple juice concentrate in a blender and blend until a puree is formed. Add tomato paste, vinegar, pepper, red pepper flakes, cinnamon, and cloves. Blend until ketchup is smooth.

Store in refrigerator in a tightly covered jar.

Ketchup will keep several months in the refrigerator.

Yield: Approximately 1 1/2 cups

DRINKS

CHOCOLATE MALTED MILK SHAKE

5 large scoops chocolate ice cream or ice milk
1 1/2 cups milk
1 tablespoon malted milk powder
2 tablespoons chocolate syrup

Combine all ingredients in a blender and blend thoroughly.

Yield: 2 servings

VANILLA MILK SHAKE

5 large scoops vanilla ice cream or ice milk
1 1/2 cups milk
1 1/2 teaspoons vanilla
1 teaspoon sugar

Combine all ingredients in a blender and blend thoroughly.

Yield: 2 servings

STRAWBERRY-BANANA MILK SHAKE

4 scoops vanilla ice cream or ice milk
1 very ripe banana
1 1/2 cups milk
1 teaspoon vanilla
2 fresh strawberries
2 mint leaves

Combine ice cream, banana, milk, and vanilla in a blender and blend thoroughly.

Garnish with strawberries and mint leaves.

Yield: 2 servings

HONEY-PEANUT BUTTER MILK SHAKE

4 scoops vanilla ice cream or ice milk
1/2 cup creamy peanut butter
1 1/2 cups milk
1/2 teaspoon ground cinnamon
1 tablespoon honey

Combine all ingredients in a blender and blend thoroughly.

Yield: 2 servings

DANNY "THE SELTZER MAN" MANCHER'S OLD-FASHIONED NEW YORK EGG CREAM

¹/₄ cup chocolate syrup
¹/₂ cup milk
³/₄ cup seltzer

Put chocolate syrup into a 12-ounce glass and add milk, stirring well.

Add seltzer and stir again.

If you are lucky enough to have a real seltzer bottle, add the seltzer by placing a spoon in the glass and direct the flow of the seltzer onto the spoon rather than directly into the milk. This will minimize the amount of foam that is formed.

Yield: 1 serving

INDEX

Apple Apricot Chutney, 101
Avo-Burger-Cado, 53

Bacon and Mozzarella Burgers, 57
Bacon-Cheeseburger, 4
Baked Beer Burgers, 31
Barbecue Burger Sauce, 46
Barbecue Burgers, 34
Basic Burger, Your, 3
Basic Cheeseburger, Your, 4
Beef and Liver Burgers, 65
Beefburger Reuben, 49
Brandy Burgers, 52
Brew-Fried Onion Rings, 92
Burger Royale, 14
Burgers Italiano, 39

California Burger, 13
Caraway Burgers, 38
Cheese-Braised Onions, 93
Chili Cheeseburgers, 37
Chocolate Malted Milk Shake, 105
Colby and Onion Burger, 24
Cordon Bleu Hamburgers, 33
Corn Relish, 100
Craig Claiborne's Hamburgers, 12
Cranberry-Curry Burgers, 51
Crispy Potato Skins, 81
Cucumber and Onion Salad, 88
Curried Oat Hamburgers, 35

Danny "The Seltzer Man" Mancher's
   Old-Fashioned New York Egg
   Cream, 107
Diane's Macaroni Salad, 86
Dr. Joyce Brothers's Meat Loaf, 15
Dom DeLuise's Meatballs, 16

Egg Potato Salad, 85

Family Favorite Rolls, 76
Fishburgers, 67
Fried Mushrooms, 95

Garnished Steak Tartare, 55
Good and Spicy Ketchup, 102
Grilled Parmesan Burgers, 28

Hamburg Steaks, 11
Hamburger Buns: Plain & Fancy, 75
Hamburger Egg Surprise, 29
Hamburgers en Croûte, 32
Healthy Hamburgers, 45
Heritage "Maytag Blue" Burger, 19
Hoagieburgers, 50
Homemade French-Fried Potatoes,
   82
Homemade Potato Chips, 83
Honey-Peanut Butter Milk Shake,
   106
Hot Chili con Carne Burgers, 25
Hot Dog Burgers, 66

Lamburgers, 70

Marge's Cole Slaw, 89
Marinated Mushrooms, 94
Marinated Veal Burger Sandwiches,
   63
Mild Tomato Pepper Relish, 99

Nana's Special Sour Cream Potato
   Salad, 84
Noodleburgers, 64
Nutty Burgers, 48

Onion Surprise Hamburgers, 36
Oriental Burgers, 43

Pita Bread, 77
Pizza Burgers, 27

Ranch Sauce, 40
Rice and Walnut Salad, 87
Rice Noodle Sauce, 54
Roquefort and Wine Burgers, 23

Sauerbraten Burgers, 41
Scallion Butter Burgers, 44
Scandinavian Burgers, 56
Sloppy Joes, 46
Snappyburgers, 30
Spiced Turkeyburgers, 61
Sprout Burgers in Pita Pockets, 54
Strawberry-Banana Milk Shake, 106
String Bean Vinaigrette, 90

Stuffed Bacon-Cheeseburgers, 42
Superlative Hamburger Sauce Diane,
  18
Sweet Pickle Hamburger, 26

Taco Pita Pockets, 47
Tangy Chickenburgers, 62
Thousand Island Dressing, 49
Three-Bean Bacon Bake, 91
Tofu Burgers, 69
Tomato and Ginger Sauce, 30
Truffle Shallot Burger, The, 17

Vanilla Milk Shake, 105
Veggieburgers, 68

Western Hamburgers, 40